TAKE A BOW DOBBYDOO

By

Chris Marczak

Mom, Dad, Julie, Joe, Kevin, and Evan thank you for always having my back. Lizzy, Nick, Marshall, and Cadence for being the extra sparkle in our world. Pamela and Kim for walking the path with us that led to this book. Thank you; we love you all!

This book is dedicated to anyone who is brave enough to try. And, anyone that has adopted, fostered, or donated. -Thank you!

Copyright ©Chris Marczak 2016

All rights reserved. This work, all the photographs and written text contained therein, are the intellectual property of the author and are protected by the US and international copyright laws. No part of this book may be reproduced or transmitted in any form by an means graphic, electronics, or mechanical, including photographs, recording or taping, or by any informational storage retrieval system without written permission of the author.

Take A Bow DobbyDoo

By

Chris Marczak

Not everyone has an easy start to life. That was true for DobbyDoo the boxer.

Dobby was born to a family that; for whatever reason, could not keep him. He was taken to a place that finds new homes for pets in need.

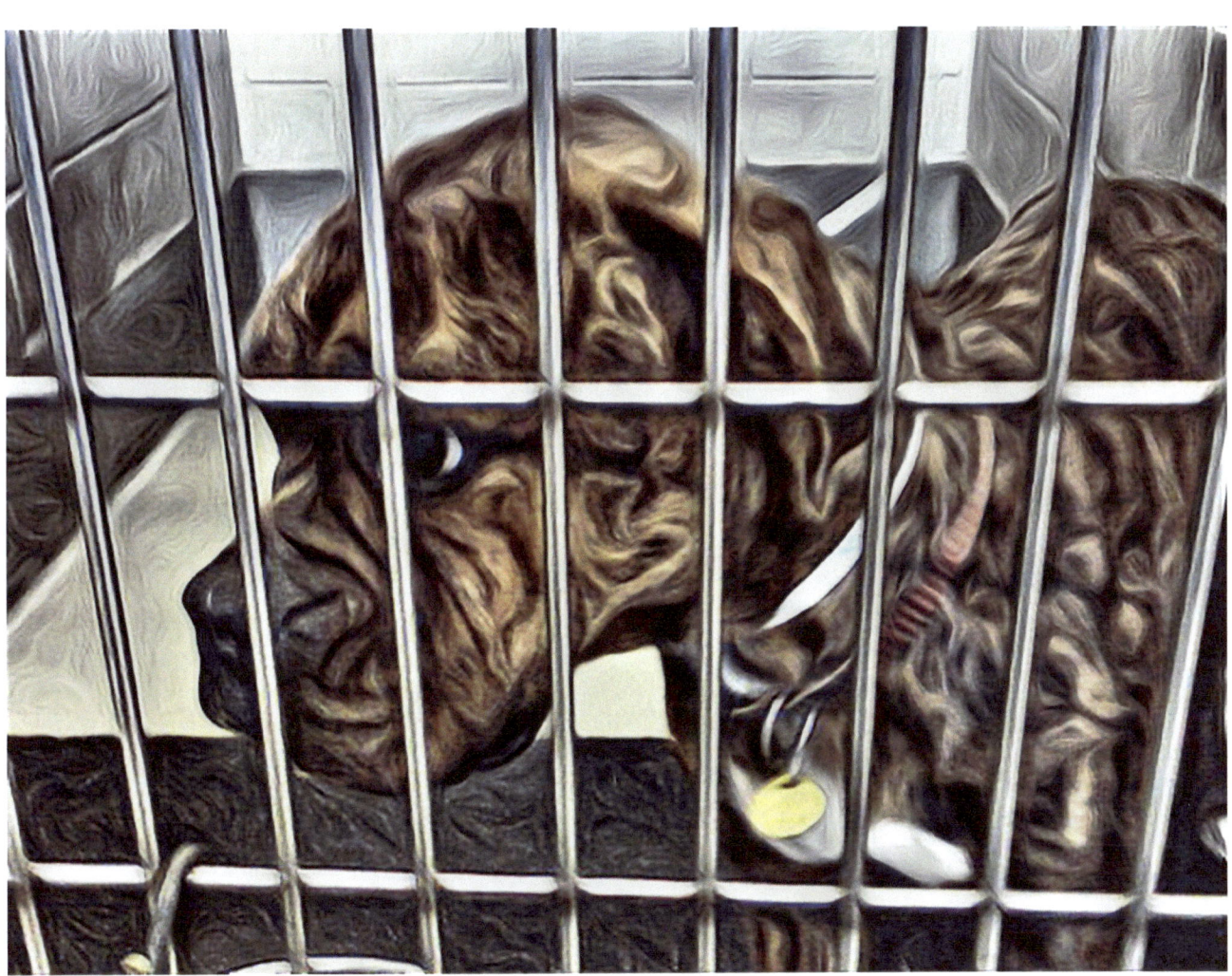

Dobby was adopted. Dobby's new family was just he and his furless mom, but he didn't care because he was loved.

His new mom wanted him to run and jump, but DobbyDoo could not. He was born with misshapen hips. Because of this he could not do all the things other dogs could do.

Dobby's mom learned about a school that could teach him special manners. DobbyDoo liked these new manners.

He learned; no jumping on people, never be mean, and how to get along with everyone.

People would pet him and give him lots of affection.

He had to take a test to show that he had learned his manners.

Now that he graduated DobbyDoo could do and go places that other dogs could not.

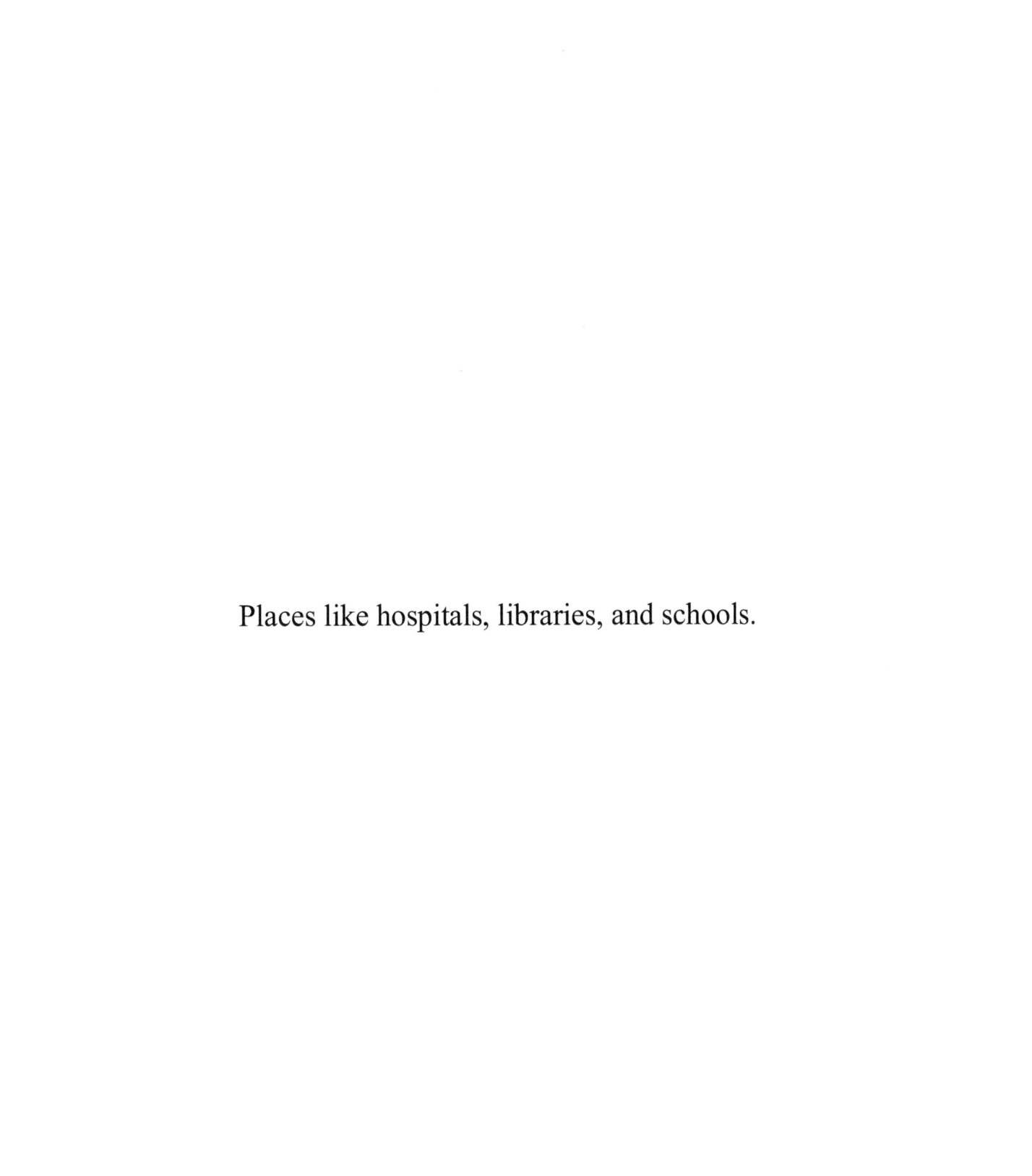

Places like hospitals, libraries, and schools.

Dobby now has a job. He is helping kids learn how to read.

His job is to listen to kids read to him.

Listen to the mistakes. Listen to the accidents.

Listen to the fumbles, bumbles, and tumbles that can happen when learning how to read.

Dobby's job is not to say anything or judge how well they are doing. He just listens.

He listens to the changes, the progress and the growth that happens. He listens as kids improve and become better readers.

DobbyDoo loves his job!

He didn't have the best start in life, but that doesn't matter.

What does matter is that he became the best that he could be and is doing a great job.

He has helped lots of kids learn to read. Job well done!

TAKE A BOW DOBBYDOO!

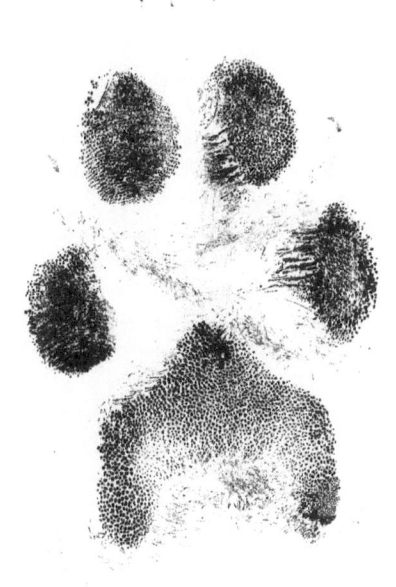

www.ingramcontent.com/pod-product-compliance
Lightning Source LLC
Chambersburg PA
CBHW041534040426
42446CB00002B/87